Essence of Tawhid

Denial of Servitude But to God

Sayyid 'Alī Ḥusaynī Khāmina'ī

AL-BURĀQ

Copyright

ISBN: 978-1-956276-23-7
Printed and published by al-Burāq Publications.

Ordering Information
We offer discounts and promotions for wholesale purchases, non-profit organizations, and other educational institutions. Contact us at the email below for further information.

www.al-Buraq.org
publications@al-Buraq.org

First Edition | January 2019
Second Edition | July 2022

Dedication

The publication of this book was made possible through the generous support of our donors.

Please recite *Sūrat al-Fātiḥa* and ask God for the Divine reward (*thawāb*) to be conferred upon the donors and also the souls of all the deceased in whose memory their loved ones have contributed graciously towards the publication of *Essence of Tawhid: Denial of Servitude But to God.*

Duʿā' al-Ḥujjah

O God, be, for Your representative, the
Ḥujjat (proof), son of al-Ḥasan, Your
blessings be upon him and his forefathers,
in this hour and in every hour: a guardian,
a protector, a leader, a helper, a proof, and
an eye - until You make him live on the
Earth, in obedience (to You), and cause
him to live in it for a long time.

In the Name of God, the Beneficent, the Merciful

The Prophet of Islam announced a slogan: "There is no god but Allah" - a pedestal in his profound message towards emancipation of man. The chieftains and the nobles of the tribes were the prime figures who rose in an alarm to confront him. In the beginning only mocking and censuring served to them as a primitive tool of animosity which later turned into so-called effective weapons in line with the progress of the movement of Tawhid (Divine Unity). The others under their influence were also goaded into enmity towards the Prophet and his believers. Here, the shameful episodes of history took place stretching a span of thirteen years which preceded the migration. This historical reality reveals a fact which deserves a cogent consideration towards a re-acquaintance of Islam and specially Tawhid (an essential word of Islam, its first and its final).

One of the most pitiful events of our days is the distorted concept of Tawhid; and this should be regarded as a tragedy by all those who have a say in emancipation of man, because of the bearing of this distortion on the common and most fundamental concept of all the religions, as there cannot be found any other concept in the expanse of history that could have been so efficacious in the course of emancipation of man besides its being a harbinger of redemption for the oppressed masses.

In history, as far as we have known, the divinity prophecies were movements momentous towards the benefit of mankind, freeing the oppressed ones against atrocities, discrimination and encroachments.

The moral core of all the great religions according to Erich Fromm includes such ideals as: knowledge, brotherly love, minimizing human sufferings, independence and responsibility (Of course, comprehension of ideals still nobler, cannot be expected from a materialist observer). Indeed all these ideals are epitomized in Tawhid. Prophets while exposing their errand in the slogan, focusing at Tawhid, were translating it into reality, following the campaign issued by this slogan. It is, indeed, deplorable for those who believe in Tawhid and its outlook upon universe and those who are after the above ideals that the concept of Tawhid should remain unknown or become an enigma or else perverted or if at all conceived should not go beyond a cursory conception that too merely a mental one at a time when the said ideals are felt more and sought faster than ever.

The earlier confrontations that started with the dawn of Islam reveal an important fact with regards the concepts of Tawhid. That fact is this: the slogan, "There is no god but Allah", was in the very first place a blow fatal to those who had gritted their teeth of enmity against it and it were they the ruling class of the society with due power. The social orientation of a movement or a thought and the efficiency of such orientation can well be conceived through the adversary reactions to that movement or thought. The very faces of the enemies of a movement will well disclose, upon a study, the nature of their affiliations with social stratum and thereby the confrontation of that society as a whole in relation to that particular movement or thought. The strength of the enmity is the gauge that determines the strength of the movement. Thus, the study of both the wings - one that of the supporters of the movement and the other that of its adversaries - becomes safe and sane to gain a true acquaintance with the Divine movements.

When we observe that those classes that are puissant in society have been the first to confront the call of religions and to do this they have done the best they could afford, we clearly realize that a religion or any religious movement in its nature is against these classes; it opposes to their lavishing either in power or in pelf, and basically to any classification that distinguishes them from others.

To ponder into the very concept of Tawhid from this angle, the angle of its opposition to the majesty over the society, we should necessarily know that Tawhid is not a mere theory either that of a philosophy or a noetic one, as it is a general error in common presumption; but it is the very foundation whereupon is edified man and the mammoth mansion of the universe in addition to its being a social, economical and political doctrine too.

In the terminology of religion, or among other terms, a term could hardly be found to the extent that could be so fertile as to enfold so much of the revolutionary and constructive concepts, besides covering different aspects of man's social and historical life. It could, therefore, never be just fortuitous that all the

Divine solicitations and Divine movements that are so profuse in history did hint and hit at one point, in their proclamations, and that is the Oneness of God and the Divinity is only His and to Him alone.

To describe the rays that a prism of Tawhid imparts, we could only epitome:

1. From the Point of View of its General Outlook upon the Universe:

a. It translates to the effect of a united world and homely uniformity of all its elements. Since the Creator is one, and everything is originated from one source, since there have not been different gods and creators, creating and then running the world, then all the things are elements of one set and the whole world is one unit with one pursuit. God the Almighty challenges:

"Thou seest not in the creation of the All-merciful any disorder." (al-Mulk, 67:3)

Again says the Almighty:

"What, have they not considered within themselves? God created not the heavens and the earth, and what is between them, but on a just system, and with a stated term." (ar-Rum, 30:8)

From this outlook, the world appears a caravan with a set-up connected to each other like a chain and heading towards one direction in unison with a common conquest so well organized that every item is carefully placed in its due position; or else it might have lost its usefulness. Thus, all are in a journey compact, consistent, constant towards consummation; each a necessity to the other while the rest rests on such a need as a whole thereby avoiding any sluggishness or deviation which, otherwise, would consequent in an upset of this whole set-up.

b. Tawhid can also be translated to the objectivity of the creation, and the planning and computed order in the world; to the existence of some sort of dynamism and purpose in all and each part of the world. Since the universe has a wise (wise in its most complete sense that could be a deserving description of the word Hakim [a name among the names of Allah]) Creator Who has brought it into existence, there is no way but being a wisdom, an ultimate purpose, and a pursuit in the very existence of the world as it is seen and sensed in most of its parts.

"We created not the heaven and the earth, and whatsoever is between them, as playing and with no purpose." (al-Ambiya', 21:16)

From this outlook the world seems to be a machine manufactured for a gain and not a thing lost in a wilderness of bewilderment. The very fact as to how it is, purports a meaning and portrays a purpose which is not to be sought in the origin. It is like a verse that can only be understood by probing into its content but never can be considered its existence as a matter of chance.

c. Tawhid, moreover cognates to obedience of all the things and the elements of the world before God. Neither a thing nor a regulation in this galaxy is at its own. The rules that run the world and everything existing under their guidance are all into a constant obeisance to the divinity of God. Therefore, existence of the rules and laws in this whole world cannot be considered as a reason to deny God's presence, divinity and His constant control over the world.

In this respect the Holy Qur'an says:

"None is there in the heavens and the earth but he comes to the All-merciful as a servant." (Maryam, 19:93)

"But to Him is what in the heavens and (in) the earth - all to Him (are) obedients." (al-Baqarah, 2:116)

"They measured not God with His true measure. The earth altogether shall be His handful on the Day of Resurrection, and the heavens shall be rolled up in His right hand. Glory be to Him! He exalted above that they associate!" (az-Zumar, 39:67)

2. From the Outlook Consequented upon Studying and Judgment on Man:

a. It is in the sense of the uniformity and equality of human beings in relation to God. He is the Master of all people. Human nature is so even that it rescinds any particularity in his relation with God. No one has any kinship with Him. Hence, all are same and at parity before God. Also God is not a particular one of a particular nation or a group or a tribe; and, therefore, the absence of superior avoids the notion of inferior in the creation while leaves open the scope for elevation of the human values which is attainable only through righteousness, a platform whereon to perform good deeds in line with Divine's desire which is the only safe route or promising method for man to ascend to heights of perfection and prosperity. To quote from the Qur'an:

"And they said, 'God has taken to Him a son'. Glory be to Him! Nay, to Him belongs all that is in the heavens and the earth; all obey His will." (al-Baqarah, 2:117)

"And whosoever does deeds of righteousness, being a believer, no unthankfulness shall befall his endeavor; We ourselves write it down for him." (al-Ambiya', 21:94)

"O Mankind! We have created you male and female, and appointed you races and tribes, that you

may know one another. Surely the noblest among you in the sight of God is the most God-fearing of you."
(al-Hujarat, 49:13)

b. It is also in the sense that man is equal in creation and is originated from a single source, this equality also runs in the very vitality of human beings. Those who belong to the various classes in a society are not created by different gods. Humanity is a single element that has been equally given to all individuals. So there is no difference in the pulp or in the creation provided to them. As such, there is no boundary between them that cannot be crossed. In other words, the Creator of the higher classes of society is not a God superior than that of the poor ones. All are created by one God and in creation all are at the same level and equally benefited from the element of humanity. To quote from the Qur'an:

"O mankind! Fear your Lord, Who created you of a single soul." (an- Nisa', 4:1)

c. The equality among the human beings carries the same bearing upon the possibility of elevation and perfection of individuals too. The obvious reason is that the human gist is the same in all men while taking its root from one wisdom. This being so, no one is impuissant in his nature not to be able to pace the path of perfection. Accordingly, the Divine call is common to all irrespective of nations or classes. To quote from the Qur'an:

"We have sent thee not [to a special group] except to mankind, entire." (Saba', 34:29)

"And We have sent thee for the people a messenger." (an-Nisa', 4:79)

"O men, a clear guide has now come to you from your Lord; We have sent down to you a manifest light. As for those who believe in God, and hold fast to Him, He will surely admit them to mercy from Him, and bounty, and will guide them to Him on a straight path." (an-Nisa', 4:174,175)

d. It can also be translated to the release of all human beings from servitude and yielding to anyone but God. This is another interpretation of the essence of complete yielding to God and worshipping Him. Some people, in some way or other, have yielded to the obscene yoke of submission to other than God', such as mental, cultural, economical, and political slavery. Considering the wide stretching sense of worship, we can well say that they are immured in service to others - like themselves - and, thus, have taken a rival or an associate to God. Here, Tawhid totally rejects such a way of life and stands firm and adamant to maintain the man a servant to God alone and emancipates him from that domination, under whatever pretext it be. Therefore, Tawhid is tantamount to denial 'of any power concealed under whatever colour or cloak, and an absolute submission to the absolute authority of God alone. To quote from the Qur'an:

"Authority belongs only to God; He has commanded that you shall not serve and worship any but Him. That is the right religion". (Yusuf, 12:40)

"Thy Lord has decreed you shall not serve and worship any but Him." (al-Isra', 17:23)

e. As such Tawhid is to dignify man, the worth of man is so lofty that to become servile and resigned to others (but to God), and get dominated is in immediate contrast. an obvious opposition and a crisp contradiction with that worth.

There is no one to countenance this worth so as to be servile to him except God. He is the only Being, the only perfect Pulchritude in absoluteness that deserves a man to sit in an enchantment of praise and prayer to Him. The kingdom of God in the vast human fife is invaded without a right and inroads are made upon the intellect of man by those idols - the living ones or the made-up ones who are, in fact, a product of evil while themselves wicked enough to throw the man from the zenith of humanity into the abyss of vileness discarding the human value and invalidating its worth. It is upon man to shun from the shame of worshipping servitude to them.

Materialistic humanism has never been able to establish the originality of man in its due excellence with a delicacy that dashes into the depth and a lofty sense splashes therefrom, such as:

"And eschew the abomination of idols, and eschew the speaking of falsehood, being men pure of faith

unto God, not associating with Him anything; for whosoever associates with God anything, it is as though he has fallen from heaven and the birds snatch him away, or the wit7d sweeps him headlong into a place far away." (al-Hajj, 22:30, 31)

"Set not up with God another god, or thou wilt sit condemned and forsaken." (al- Isra', 17:22)

"Set not up with God another god, or thou wilt sit cast into hell, reproached and rejected." (al-Isra', 17:39).

f. In this category another meaning of Tawhid is that, a human life is a compound of mind and reality, thought and action. If one of these two, or partially both, got dominated by the anti-Divine powers; in other words, if the intellect lenient to God with an undivine reality, or a Divine desired reality with an intellect ignorant of God becomes espoused, then in the kingdom of human life duality has occurred and thus an associate is created in the servitude directed to God. In this case, the example of man will be like that of a needle, being in a magnetic field, besides the earth's one, if not deviated totally from the pole direction he would be oscillating. Deviation shall dictate departure from a straight path of God and shall doom him to a destiny that is not his.

To quote from the Qur'an:

"What do you believe in part of the Book, and disbelieve in other part? What shall be the recompense of those of you who do that, but degradation in the present life, and on the Day of Resurrection to be returned unto the most terrible chastisement?" (al Baqarah, 2:85)

g. And finally, Tawhid, from this point of view translates the human coordination coherent with the universal milieu. The stintless vastness of the expanse of the universe is a ground wherein innumerous laws of creation are in action and reaction and so constant that any product of the universe, however small and little or trivial and trifle, cannot escape from the dart of the rays of this law. The law of creation is set on a keyboard of traditions and the strokes thereon is such a mercy as to bring out into audience a tune titivated with tucket in full tilt of the gamut of existence and thereby comes into being the pleasing and the portentous display of the universe that embraces the man too in its parcel so packed therein as to obey a general law while enjoying a law particular to himself; and, thus, remain congruous to the consequences as a whole. Indeed, the salient characteristic in a man (in contradiction to his other fellow creatures who pace towards their natural destiny with no choice) is his being open to option and his power to practice his choice - a criterion for his ascendancy to excellence and as well as a ground to go astray. To quote from the Qur'an:

"So let whosoever will believe, and let whosoever will disbelieve." (al-Kahf, 8:29)

Tawhid solicits the man to pace the way natural to him and congenial with- the universe. Man as he is the main part of this whole gets attached by his trudge in his pace and here consequents an absolute parity and a total oneness. To quote from the Qur'an:

"What, do they desire another religion than God's, and to Him has surrendered whoso is in the heavens

and the earth, willingly or unwillingly, and to Him
they shall be returned." (Ali-Imran, 3:83)

"Hast thou not seen how to God bow all who are in
the heavens and all who are in the earth; the sun and
the moon, the stars and the mountains, the trees and
the beasts, and many of mankind?" (al-Hajj, 22:18)

3. The Outlook from the Social, Economical, and Political Stands:

a. In the affairs, those of universal and those of human, the competency is to none besides God. Planning, whatsoever, and an independent direction is only to the competency of the Creator Who is All-knowing and Allaware of the needs and the possibilities. The hidden treasures of talents in a human body as well as those innumerable ones in the vast of the universe together with the relative potentialities in addition to the places of their display, and, furthermore, the conjugation in between them; all are in His sight and never apart from His wisdom.

Therefore, it is He alone, the competent one, to fashion the life and plan a schedule of relations for man which is again at parity with the line of his pace in the system of the galaxy; and accordingly a system to be sketched for a society, it rests finally on His competency. This right (as described above) is particularly His and to Him alone, because of the natural and logical consequence of His being God - the Almighty, the Creator, the Master. Therefore, any sort of interference from any in determination of a line to be practiced by a man or a destiny to be headed to, is an encroachment into the kingdom of Divinity and an inroad into the intrinsic exalted excellence of Divine. Thus, it is polytheism. To quote from the Qur'an:

"But no, by thy Lord! They will not believe till they make thee the judge regarding the disagreement between them, then they shall find in themselves no impediment touching thy verdict, but shall surrender in full submission." (an-Nisa, 4:65)

"It is not for any believer, man or woman, when God and His Messenger have decreed a matter, to have the choice in the affair. Whosoever disobeys God and His Messenger has gone astray into manifest error."
(al-Ahzab 33:36)

b. The right of guardianship and supervision of a society and the leadership of a human life is rejected but to God. Government or a guardianship of a man over a man would necessarily carry tyranny as a concomitant; If considered as an independent right bare of any responsibility unless the leadership and supervision over the social affairs should be given by a higher power to an individual or vested into a ruling committee coasted with congenial responsibilities; then alone the recalcitrations, obstructions obumbrated by intransigence could only be leveled and slaked. According to the ideology of the religion such a might is Allah, whose knowledge has no bourne. To quote from the Qur'an:

"Not so much as the weight of (even) an atom in heaven and earth escapes from Him" (Saba 34:3)

His dudgeon among His qualities (Mighty Punisher, Strong Revenger) leaves no room for any deviation for His chosen and appointed ones. To quote from the Qur'an.

"Had he invented against Us any sayings, We would have seized him by the right hand, then We would surely have cut his life-vein." (al-Haqqah, 69:44-46)

The government of God is not like one appointed by a nation nor a majority that could be fooled and run, nor a party that could be abused as a means for oppressing and pushing the people's voice down. It is not like the one appointed by the aristocrats and wealth holders of the society that could be bribed or accepted as shareholders of their enterprises. To ponder further deep: if human life is indentured to terminate at a point along with all its accessory organizations and the thread of the things to be held by a most puissant hand - as it is, of course - then such a hand could never be but that of the Creator's. As such, it is a right especial to God Himself to govern the man which He does through those whom He appoints, those are best in line according to the standards established in Divine ideology. So, it is they who carry out the Divine decrees as they guard.

To quote from the Qur'an:

"Say: 'Shall I take a guardian and a ruler other than God, the Originator of the heavens and of the earth, He who feeds and is not fed?' Say: 'I have been commanded to be the first of them that surrender to the command of God." And you should not be among those of the idolators." (al-An'am, 6:14)

Your guardian (authority) is only God, and His Messenger and those who believed, who perform the prayer and pay the alms while they bow down (in their prayer)." (al-Maidah, 5:55)

"Say: 'I take refuge with the Lord of men, the ruler of men, the God of men.'" (an-Nas, 114:2-4)

c. Absolute possession and provenance of all the bounties and the stocks existing in the world goes to the belonging of God. Nothing is in an independent belonging of any in this world although everything in the use of man is a deposit from Divine so as to be beneficial towards the perfection and elevation of man. This is not in the sense that a man is at his own convenience to spoil - if he wished - the bounties of this world which, as a matter of fact, are the result of the toil of innumerous hands. Man is also not at liberty to enjoy the utilization of these bounties in the errands other than those of his own elevation.

Whatever is available for man, although for him, is given by God, therefore, should be utilized for what God (the Donor) has specified and willed, and in fact, should be used in its main and natural way. It should be benefited from in the same manner that it is created for. Consuming it in any other way is a deviation from its real use consequenting in evil. The role of man in this display of different and colourful bounties of God, is to utilize them in the right way; of course with first and foremost aim at their own perfection. To quote from the Qur'an:

"Say: 'Whose is the earth, and whoso is in it; if you have knowledge?' They will say: 'God's. 'Say: 'Will you not then remember?" (al-Mu'minun, 84, 85)

"It is He Who created for you mankind all that is in the earth. " (al-Baqarah, 2:29) "Serve God! You have no god other than He. It is He Who produced you from the earth and has given you to live therein."
(Hud, 11:61)

"And those who break the covenant if God after His compact, and who snap what God has commanded to be joined, and who work corruption in the earth, theirs shall be the curse... " (ar-Ra'd, 13:25)

d. The right in relation with the bounties of the world is at parity among men. The opportunities and the possibilities are equally open to all. Every man is quite free to have his share in congruity with the endeavor that he exerts. In this stintless expanse there is no precinct prescribed particularly to a person as there are no divisions such as those of creed, geographical, historical, and even ideological. All are in an open to toil and take their share. To quoted from the Qur'an:

"It is He Who created for you all [and not for a particular section of you] in the earth,"(al-Baqarah, 2:29)

"And the cattle, He created them for you; in them is warmth, and uses of various, and of them you eat. And there is beauty in them for you, when you bring them home to rest and when you drive them forth

> *abroad to pasture. And they carry your heavy loads..." (an-Nahl, 16:5-7)*

> *"it is He Who sends down to you out of heaven water." (an-Nahl, 16:10)*

> *"Thereby He brings forth for you crops...." (an-Nahl, 16:11)*

> *"And what He has created in the earth...." (an-Nahl, 16:13)*

> *"God is He Who made for you the cattle that you may ride on some of them, and of them you may eat." (Ghafir, 40:79)*

In these verses of the beginning of the chapter, an-Nahl, (The Bees), the address is to men and not to any particular group.

The same can be seen in other phrase among the same verses:

> *"If He willed He guides you all..." (an-Nahl, 16:9)*

> *"Your God is one God..." (an-Nahl, 16:22)*

So far our discourse covers only a little of this uberous dimensions of the rich and deep concept of Tawhid. This little yet sufficiently ratiocinates that Tawhid is not a mere philosophical or noetic impracticable theory, that in no way does it care about the man's way of life, and nor interferes in determination of man's destiny as to what and how he acts to reach it. It is not just to substitute people's belief. But it is a way for comprehension of the universe. It gives a particular understanding of the universe and the man, of the position of man in cognition to other beings in the world, of the man's position in history, of his capabilities and needs which are always in him and with him, and finally of the direction and the high perch of his perfection.

On the other hand, it is a social doctrine. It is a design and sketch of the environment ideonous to man wherein he can easily progress towards perfection. It is a mould meant for the society, fixes a basical line and forwards a constructive principle. Whenever a society sinks into ignorance and tyranny and loses the character that is the distinction of man, the principle is there to check. It is a relief to ailing hearts, a frill to a fallen and a typhoon in a stagnant, marsh of the society so that it could rebuild itself; and it is such a change as to dislodge the foundations and wrench the stones from stones of the social and economical wrong setups, rescinds the value while reveals the true worth.

In short, it is a protest in every constancy against the existing conditions contrived by tyranny. Tawhid is not a new answer nor with infinitude of practice. It is a way ever new and always green for a man. Although it leans to a theoretical and mental analysis, its main goal is to provide another method for man's active life. Therefore, we believe that Tawhid is the radex of religion and a cornerstone whereon rests the pillars of its mansion. It holds a mammoth ideology, the backbone of Islam, as a social conduct. It is not just a delicate body to house a thesis of a moral or a judgment of a metaphysics.

There have always been those who in spite of their belief in God and Tawhid, have neglected the obvious, practical and specially social aspects of this belief, either deliberately or otherwise. These easy believers - regardless of circumstances - have always dwelt a life like that of non-believers; and their belief has ever been at failure to suscitate any feeling in them that could forbid from inhaling the putridity of the polytheism. During the dawn of Islam in

Mecca, the capital of the renown idols of Arabs, there were also the supporters of lbrahim's (Abraham's) upright religion. But Tawhid was so confined in their minds that its utmost influence was only limited to their individual conduct. Neither their presence curbed nor their absence gave reins to the conjectures of their society; such weightless was their existence and so it continued without ebb and flow.

Furthermore, they, the socalled believers, let themselves adrift in the same current of life wherein the non-believers were at float and were carried away by the lashes of the waves of the prevailing nefarious traditions. As such, in social sphere their role was nothing; upon society itself their existence was of no effect; and in the circumstance their presence was of no influence at all. So, what else could mirror best' the characteristic of Tawhid, the interpretation of which does not surpass the mind. It was in such conditions that Islam introduced Tawhid - of course, as a thought, and the thought as strong as to promise, and the promise as fertile as to produce a frame that fringes the life and, as for society, give a new vogue and combs its disturbed hairs into a curled and crisp order.

So, with such a thought and such a promise it set foot on the ground of practice. Its very first pace revealed an invitation and the invitation disclosed a revolution which so distant and common that stunned its audience alike those who entertained, those who spurned - but all concurred in one thing that it was a Message with a new social, economical, political regulation and with a strange stubbornness to agree with the existing conditions. It denies a situation and determines another one!

Believers accepted the Message because of its clarity and openness. For this very reason, its opponents attacked it wildly and anxiously adding their pressure day by day. This fact in history is the gage to determine the veracity of those who claim Tawhid; they are no better than their peers prior to Islam - no matter in what distance of events or at what spot of the place be they, their belief is no more than a bedlam. It cannot be but a fiction or a fake of the real Tawhid focused by the apostles, if it were to see eye to eye with the rivals of God. There never existed Tawhid in such a sense. From this vista we can see the expansion of Islam in its earlier stages and judge the reactionary backwardness in later stages.

The Prophet of Islam brought Tawhid to be the way for the people. Later, it became a matter to be debated. It was a new reckoning for the world. But it was turned into a topic to beguile the time. It was the skeleton of the structure of society, and the axel in the centre of all social, economical and political affairs; but later turned into a means of justifying the existing social structure, and still remains as an axel but only in some artistic and beautiful painting of social relations, and nothing in effective existence. How can we expect an active and constructive role from a just ceremonial idea?

From the preceding discourse it comes to light that Tawhid from a practical point of view is a mould for society while a method for life, and, as a whole, an Islamic system for the human life cogent towards the progress - and this forward march is only possible in the wealth of its shade. Also from a theoretical point of view, it is an idea which is considered to be the base and philosophical foundation of that system, and a justification and reasoning for it. With this ground in the fore and in the hind, we can revert back to the starting point of the essay and analyse the subject from a particular angle, that this article is viewing at. We said the prime adversary to the slogan of Tawhid was the wealthy and the powerful class of the society.

This evinces that the first and foremost blow of Tawhid is directed against the powerful and dominating forces of society - in the Qur'anic term, the arrogant (mustakbir) class. Also we said that the Divine calls of Tawhid made clear their stand in relation to the oppressor and dominating forces as soon as they became audible in society. Therefore, the Divine calls had to face two confrontations, one opposing the other, from two antipodal wings of society: recalcitration from the oppressors (mustakbirin) and acceptance from the oppressed (mustad'afin). At last, we said that such a two sided reaction is, in fact, the characteristic of Tawhid. It is an irrefragable fact that whenever Tawhid had been or is proclaimed in its true sense, the reaction had been or will be the same.

Now, let us see which dimension among its several ones hidden in the concept of Tawhid, is in direct contrast with the interests of the oppressors? In other words, the class of oppressors do see a point in Tawhid; what is that point they are so much perturbed, and therefore, fight with such a determination ? To recognize the oppressor in the Qur'an, shall be a great help toward comprehending this subject: Mustakbir in the Qur'an. The Qur'an describes, on more than forty occasions, particulars of an oppressor from different angles such as: psychological, social Position, indulgence in power, post, and pelf. Studying the Qur'anic view of an oppressor we find him to have such characteristics as:

a. Although he (the oppressor) accepts God as a mental or ceremonial reality, or anything with a limited province, he rejects God as is described by the concept of the slogan, "There is no god but Allah." (The concept of his absolute and exclusive authority and ownership.) To quote from the Qur'an:

"For when it was said to them, 'There is no god but Allah' they were ever waxing proud." (as-Siffat, 37:35)

b. An oppressor considers himself above others and without having a rightful distinction. He declares such reasons as power and wealth to prove his claim:

> *"They waxed proud in the earth without right (to justify their position), and they said, 'Who is stronger than we in might?"* *(Fussilat, 41:15)*

c. Insisting in his false claim, he rejects the God's words which declare a new order and specify true measures:

> *"And when Our signs are recited to such a man he turns away, waxing proud, as though he heard them not, and in his ears were heaviness, so give him good tidings of a painful chastisement."* *(Luqman, 31:7)*

d. He brings forward excuse that,

> *"Had it been correct we might have conceived it earlier, or that God should have addressed us directly."* *This he does while believing the Call of the Prophet:* *"And the non-believers say as regards to the believers, 'If it had been taught good, they had not outstripped us to it."* *(al-Ahqaf, 46:11)*

> *"And when a sign came to them, they said, 'We will not believe until we are given the like of what God's Messengers were given."* *(al-An'dm, 6:124)*

e. The oppressor introduces the leader of the Call of Tawhid as one who indagates profit and a superiority and thus, leaning to old and reactionary traditions, tries to discredit him among the people:

"They said (to Moses), 'Art thou come to us to turn us from that we found our fathers practising, and that the domination in the land might belong to you two? We do not believe you two.'" (Yunus, 10:78)

f. Using force and tricks, and different methods o imposing and fooling an oppressor, pushing people in his path, which destinates to slavery, and unconditional servitude to him. Therefore, he forces them to resist and confront to any emancipating call.

"They [their followers on the Day of Resurrection], shall say, 'Our Lord, we obeyed our chiefs and great ones, and they led us astray from the way." (al-Ahzab, 33:67)

And the weak ones argue with the oppressors[on the Day of Resurrectionl, 'Why, we were your followers; will you avail us now against any part of the Fire?" (Ghafir, 40:47)

"Said the council of the aids of Pharaoh, 'Surely this man (Moses) is a cunning sorcerer who desires to

expel you from your land; what do you command?"
(al-A'raf, 7:109-110)

g. Finally, the oppressor comes into open and confronts the Prophet and his followers, who have uprised against the dominating order and are dedicated to a change, in a deliberate atrocious animosity and thought:

"Slain were the Men of the Pit, the fire abounding in fuel, when they were seated over it, and themselves were witnesses of what (tortures) they did with the believers." (al-Buruj, 85:4 - 7)

"And Pharaoh said (to his advisors),- 'Let me slay Moses, and let him call to his Lord (as he can). i fear that he may change your religion [which dominates the mind of the people], or that he may cause corruption (rebellion) to appear in the land."
(Ghafir, 40:26)

This was a small part of particularities and characteristics of the arrogant (oppressor) in some verses of the Qur'an. The Qur'an goes still beyond and classifies the arrogants (oppressors) in categories symbolizing each:

"Then We sent forth, after them, Moses and Aaron (Harun) to Pharaoh and his council with Our signs, but they waxed proud." (Yunus, 10:75)

"And Korah (Qarun), and Pharaoh, and Haman (Haman); and Moses came to them with the clear signs, but they waxed proud in the earth." (al-Ankabut, 29:39)

Pharaoh, all know him. Haman was his special advisor and a prime personality in the politics of Egypt after Pharaoh. The council of aids of Pharaoh are the chiefs in Pharaoh's regime who guide the affairs. Korah was a rich boarder of wealth and the keys of his wealth stores were in such a bulk that it was a matter of bodily strength to hold or carry them. In the light of these and several other such verses of the Qur'an the oppressor is he whose identity is: dominator of society, wields the political and economical power without reservation, to prolong his tyrannical power and the advantages therefrom; he even captivates the minds by imposing his ideology so as to keep riveted to the process that perishes them while provides possibility of persistence in oppression.

Therefore, there is every reason for an oppressor to fight against every call that enlightens the minds of people and instigates to any revolutionary and changing call; else he has to give up what he has gained and lose what he loves. Let us return to our original theme: How the prophets used to introduce Tawhid? Considering the method they used to bring forth this slogan, while revealing the most constitutional basics of their ideology, easily reveals what is the unbearable part in Tawhid for the oppressor. And secondly the reason of being so, and why this wing cannot bear Tawhid when it is so introduced?

We know that the slogan of Tawhid, had been the first rays of the call of all prophets. The sentence, "Say, there is no god but Allah, to prosper" is a well-known declaration of the Prophet of Islam. Also the sentence, "0 people, worship Allah, there is no god to you beside Him" , is repeated on several occasions in the Qur'an as the title of the call of the great prophets such as Nuh (Noah), Hud, Salih, Shu'ayb, etc. And we see, these slogans are focused to "denial of servitude but to God", and have introduced Tawhid from this point of view more than any.

The prophets have admonished the people who were in the slumber of ignorance and sunk in a tyrant society to not worship to any pole of power except God. The call, started, indeed as a challenge to those who used to claim being deities and masters of the people. Who does claim as such in a society ? What does it mean to fight them ? And what scene does this suggest to be the characteristic of a society promised by the prophets? To hold a belief of being a deity is repudiated. The tyrants who wield power, political and social, used to convey to the people that since they were deities they hold in themselves a part of the spirit of God.

On the other hand, the vastness of the concepts of 'worship', 'lordship', and 'divinity' in the Qur'an leads us to a conclusion that the claimers of being deities have even a wider scope in their pose and purpose. The term 'worship' ('ibadah) in the Qur'an means to surrender or yield or obey to a man or any other being unconditionally. When we have resigned ourselves without any 'why' it is tantamount to say that we have worshipped him. Accordingly, when an element of a power, whether inside us or from outside, has made us obedient and dependant and a tool to be used, we have become its 'worshippers and servants'; as it is evident from these Qur'anic verses, in the beginning of the call when Moses rebuked and censured Pharaoh:

"That is a Messing thou reproachest me with, having enslaved the Children of Israel." (ash-Shuara', 26:22)

The conversation between Pharaoh and the chiefs of his regime:

"Should we believe two human like us while their people are worshippers to us." (al-Mu'minun, 23:47)

Prophet lbrahim (Abraham) addresses his father as:

"Father, serve not Satan; surely Satan is a rebel against the All-merciful" (Maryam, 19:44)

In a general address of God directed to all human beings:

"Made / not covenant with you, children of Adam, that you should not serve Satan; surely he is a manfest foe to you. (Yasin, 36:60)

Promise of God to all human beings who have a reckoning:

"Those who eschew the serving of idols (taghut) and turn penitent to God, for them is good tidings! So give thou good tidings to My servants." (az-Zumar, 39:17)

Who criticize the faithfuls and the belief in God and in His revelations; God says to them:

"Whomsoever God has cursed, and with whom is on wrath, and made some of them apes and swines, and he who worshipped 'taghut, they are worse situated, and have gone further astray from the right way." (al-Midah, 5:60)

From these foregoing verses it comes to light that the obedience to Pharaoh and the members of his regime, and to a tyrant or to a Satan is interpreted as 'worship'. As such, in the sense of the Qur'anic term it means to follow, to resign, and to obey a power (other than God) in absoluteness; whether be it on a desire or under a pressure, and be it with or without a praise and sanctity. Anyway, one side turns to a worshipper while the other the worshipped. This concludes that the term 'divinity' and 'divine' (Allah) which is another interpretation of 'being worshipped', and 'the worshipped one' correctly translates to: In an errenously organized society wherein the people are divided into two classes, one that of oppressor and the other that of the oppressed. In other words, a dominator and a beneficiary class while the other a deprived one. This in itself is a paragon of a worshipper and the worshipped.

Such an inconsistency between the two wings of a society is an indicator that points to the deities whom worship is directed to. To know the worshipped ones and divines in historical societies, one should not look for a sacred being either of a man, animal or a thing. The cardinal ones in these societies are those who with their dependence upon the oppressors have yoked the multitudes of the oppressed ones. In such societies, polytheism is the religion. Because there are idols, worshipped ones, and divines as many as there are poles of power that rule the people, and push them in their own desired path as if they' (the people) have neither eyes nor ears and exactly know not where they stand and what they do.

Polytheism means accepting the divinity of others and obeying and worshipping them instead of God or leveling them with God. It means giving the control of life to others but God. It means surrendering to every pole of power other than God, seeking needs from them, and paving the path that they define. Tawhid is an antipode to such a polytheism. It denies all the deities and obedience to them. It calls for a campaign against their domination. It asks for discarding their help. And finally Tawhid is to be dedicated in reminding them as it hails upon hearts to pursue their provider, God. The prime slogan of all the messengers of God was that 'no' to others, and this 'yes' to God. To quote from the Qur'an:

"Indeed, We sent forth among every nation a messenger, say': 'Serve your God, and eschew taghuts [idols, anti-God forces].' " (an-Nahl,16:36)

'And We sent never a messenger before thee except that We revealed to him, saying, 'There is no god but /;so serve Me." (al-Ambiya', 21 :25)

Therefore, the messengers of God, by this slogan, have denied the corrupted and perverted system of society, and invited people to get in to a vast struggle against taghuts (oppressors) namely the guardians of the system, who had rebelled against the noble human values, those who had imposed some false values upon the people in order to keep their oppressing position. Denial of polytheism, in fact is the denial of all social, economical, and political foundations whereon the construction of that society rests and wherein the polytheism is housed as a rightful tenant and wherefrom keeps vegilence on the unstable situation. When the deities as such are denied and rejected, so, also all those who are dedicated to oppress the people and keep them down by imposing and fooling them, take a full advantage of all their capabilities to saturate their unlimited desires, are denied too. Moses, by declaring the same slogan, and in direct talk with the Lord of the worlds had openly fought Pharaoh, and denied him. It is true that the aids of Pharaoh brought up many guilts upon Moses, such as his denial of idols. But they and Pharaoh himself were aware of those lifeless idols that were just a cover and a justification for their own divinity.

"Then said the council of the regime of Pharaoh [to Pharaoh], 'Wilt thou leave Moses and his people to

work corruption in the land, and leave thee and thy gods?"' (al-A'raf,7:127)

The lifeless idols are just an excuse for imposing the divinity of live-idols. Therefore, it was quite logical that as a response to Moses' invitation towards God, the Creator of heavens and earth, the Lord of all, the Possessor of the east and the west; they treat him and his supporters to torture and death. To quote from the Qur'an:

"Said he (Pharaoh), 'if thou takest a god other than me, 1 shall surely make thee one of the imprisoned, (ashShu'ara', 26:29)

"Said he, 'We shall slaughter their sons and spare their women; surely we are triumphant over them." (al-A'raf, 7:127)

"Pharaoh said to his magicians who had believed in Moses against his wishes: I shall assuredly cut off alternately your hands and feet, then 1 shall crucify you all together." (al-A'raf, 7:123)

Such atrocities against the name of Allah, and the Messenger of Tawhid stand only because this emancipating message, means: Acceptance of God to dominate the life. Denial of all others who claim such with strife. Proud declaration of servitude to Him alone. Dependency to be cut upon all but upon Him sown. This is the essence of Tawhid, and its most flashing dimension.